SPOTTER'S GUIDE TO
WILD ANIMALS

Rosamund Kidman Cox

Illustrated by Malcolm McGregor

Additional illustrations by Craig Austin (Garden Studios), Rachel Lockwood, Chris Lyon, Andy Martin, Ian Jackson, Steven Kirk, David Quinn, Chris Shields, Sam Thompson, David Wright and Phil Weare.

SCHOLASTIC INC.

New York   Toronto   London   Auckland   Sydney
Mexico City   New Delhi   Hong Kong   Buenos Aires

Edited by Phillip Clarke and Clare Hickman.
Designed by Karen Tomlins and Joanne Kirkby.
Series designer: Laura Fearn
Cover designer: Nicola Butler
Expert consultants: Margaret Rostron and Sue Matthews
(Zoological Society of London).

The publisher would like to thank the following organizations for the
photographs: p.4-5 – © Paul A. Souders/Corbis; Cover; p.1-3, 6-9,
12-15, 18-19, 24-27, 30-31, 34-39, 44-49, 52-55 – © Digital Vision.

No part of this publication may be reproduced in whole or in part, or stored in a retrieval system,
or transmitted in any form or by any means, electronic, mechanical, photocopying, recording, or
otherwise, without written permission of the publisher. For information regarding permission,
write to Usborne Publishing Ltd., Usborne House, 83-85 Saffron Hill, London, EC1N 8RT,
England. First published in Great Britain in 2001 by Usborne Publishing Ltd.

ISBN 0-439-39736-7

Copyright © 2001, 1979 by Usborne Publishing Ltd. All rights reserved. Published by Scholastic
Inc., 555 Broadway, New York, NY 10012, by arrangement with Usborne Publishing Ltd. The
name Usborne and the device (🐝) are trademarks of Usborne Publishing Ltd. SCHOLASTIC
and associated logos are trademarks and/or registered trademarks of Scholastic Inc.

12 11 10 9 8 7 6 5 4 3   2 3 4 5 6 7 0

Printed in the U.S.A.   23

First Scholastic printing, March 2002

CONTENTS

HOW TO USE THIS BOOK

This book is an identification guide to some of the world's wild animals. A number of these creatures may be seen in the wild, but most people will probably see them only in wildlife parks or zoos.

Some people think that keeping animals in captivity is wrong. While it is true that there still are zoos that do not give animals the resources they need to be happy, many modern zoos help animal conservation by breeding creatures that are endangered in the wild. Some animals are now so rare that they can only be found in zoos.

The American bald eagle was nearly made extinct by hunting and pollution. Now it is thriving again due to conservation laws and breeding in zoos.

Each animal pictured in this book has a description telling you about it, including its measurements, a little about the way it behaves and where it comes from. A world map on page 59 shows all the areas mentioned in this book.

Sometimes both the male (♂) and female (♀) of a species are shown. If the sexes look alike, there is no symbol. There is also a small circle to tick when you have spotted an animal.

In this book, each type, or species, of animal shown is grouped with animals related to it. For example, all the big cats (lions, tigers etc.) are found together.

There is a separate grouping for nocturnal animals (animals active mainly at night). Animals that are very rare in the wild are also grouped together.

This is an example of how the animals are shown in the book.

⬇ REEVES' MUNTJAC
Male has small antlers. Holds its head low when running. Barks when alarmed. China. SH 50cm.

Where the animal is found

Measurements (explained on next page)

♂—Sex symbol

Tick when animal is spotted

WILDLIFE WEß SITES
On pages 60-61 you will find a list of some of the best Web sites about animals, wildlife conservation and zoos.

MEASUREMENTS

Different types of animal are measured in different ways to give the most useful information. In this book, for birds and most reptiles, the total body length (TL), including the tail, is given. Reptiles with shells are measured by the length of their shell (SL).

Most mammals are measured by head and body length (H&B) only (not including the tail). For hoofed mammals, the shoulder height (SH) is given.

Measurements are usually given as averages, but some are the maximum size of the animal. This often means that one sex is very much larger than the other.

Total length (TL)

Shell length (SL)

Head and body length (H&B)

Shoulder height (SH)

Total length (TL)

WILDLIFE PARKS AND ZOOS

When visiting a zoo or wildlife park, remember that animals are generally most active in the early morning or late afternoon. It is also a good idea to contact the place you intend to visit to find out about any special events they may be holding.

When you arrive, buy a map to tell you where the the different animals are. Also check the main noticeboard for details of feeding times and of any baby animals that may have been born.

Never feed the animals. They have their own special diets, and could be harmed by eating too much food or the wrong type of food.

VISITING SAFARI PARKS

If you are visiting a park where you have to travel around by car, remember to take some binoculars. This way you will be able to watch closely even nervous animals that keep their distance.

Hippos spend most of the day in the water, coming onto land to graze.

WATCHING ANIMALS

Wildlife parks and zoos are good places to study the way animals behave. You could look out for some of the features listed here.

• **Teeth** The shape and size of an animal's teeth can tell you a lot about what it eats. Look in the animal's enclosure for further clues to its diet.

• **Colour and size**
With many animals, these can provide important clues to age and sex.

• **Special adaptations**
The physical characteristics of animals often reveal their lifestyle. Many monkeys, for example, have tails that are specially adapted for grasping branches.

A lion's large canine teeth show that it is a carnivore (meat eater).

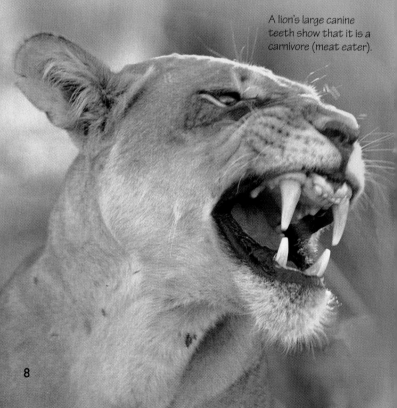

- **Sleeping position**
A number of hoofed animals, for example the giraffe, sleep standing up.

- **Group behaviour**
Animals living in groups act differently according to their position in the group's social order. The leader of a grey wolf pack, for example, shows its importance by growling and raising its ears and tail. A more lowly wolf will flatten its ears and tuck its tail between its legs to show that it knows its place.

- **Movement** The way an animal moves can yield clues to its lifestyle. A spider monkey's ability to swing, for example, tells of its life in the treetops.

Springboks are named for the agile leaping by which they escape danger.

LATIN NAMES

The sign on an animal's enclosure often shows a Latin name as well as a common name. Common names vary from place to place, but Latin names stay the same.

LION
Species: *Panthera leo*
Family: *Felidae*
Order: *Carnivora*

JUNGLE CAT
Species: *Felis chaus*
Family: *Felidae*
Order: *Carnivora*

Latin names show how animals are related. Both animals above, for example, belong to a large group, or order, called the *Carnivora* (Meat-eaters). Within this order, they both belong to the Cat family (*Felidae*). Within this family, the lion is a species, or type, among the Big Cats (*Panthera*), while the jungle cat is grouped with the Smaller Cats (*Felis*).

9

APES

➡ ORANG-UTAN
Strong but gentle.
Unlike other apes in
that it lives alone. It
prefers to sleep off
the ground. Rare.
Sumatra; Borneo.
H&B 1.4m.

⬅ LOWLAND GORILLA
Shy, gentle, intelligent
and very strong. Lives
in groups. Dominant
males are called
"silverbacks" because
of their colour. Rare.
Central W Africa.
H&B 1.5m.

*Use their front
knuckles when
walking*

➡ CHIMPANZEE
Excitable. Adult chimps
can be dangerous.
Watch how they
communicate with
facial expressions.
Rare. Central W
Africa. H&B 1m.

GIBBON, MONKEYS

Can swing along very quickly using its long arms

➡ WHITE-HANDED GIBBON
Also called a **Lar Gibbon**. It lives in pairs with its young. Moves by swinging rather than climbing. Listen for its hooting call. Rare. S-E Asia. H&B 50cm.

➡ PIG-TAILED MACAQUE
Lives in large troops. Try to spot the dominant male leader: he often pouts as a threat or greeting. S-E Asia. H&B 60cm max.

Flesh-coloured rump

♂

⬅ GELADA
The female's chest patch only turns red at mating time. An angry male flashes white eyelids and exposes his canine teeth. Ethiopia. H&B 70cm max.

⬅ MANDRILL
The male leader is the largest, and has the most brightly coloured face and rump. He sometimes barks. W Africa. H&B 80cm.

♂

MONKEYS

➡ VERVET MONKEY
In zoos, older same-sex monkeys fight. Young or parents do not. Grooming builds friendship. Africa. H&B 60cm.

➡ PATAS MONKEY
You will see it on the ground, but it sleeps in branches. Females are very possessive of their young. C & S Africa. H&B 80cm.

♂

◀ ABYSSINIAN COLOBUS
Shy. Spends most of its time in the trees. Babies may be passed around between the females. Africa. H&B 65cm.

♂

◀ PROBOSCIS MONKEY
Nose grows throughout life. The male's is longer than the female's. If alarmed, the male's nose straightens. Rare. Borneo. H&B 75cm.

SOUTH AMERICAN MONKEYS

➡ SQUIRREL MONKEY
Lives in big groups. Runs along branches on all fours, using its tail as a balance. S America. H&B 35cm.

➡ HUMBOLDT'S WOOLLY MONKEY
Has a prehensile tail which can grip branches or even grasp bits of food. S America. H&B 70cm.

♂

◀ WHITE-FACED SAKI
Easily frightened, it makes loud, bird-like alarm calls. The male helps carry the young. S America. H&B 50cm max.

➡ COMMON MARMOSET
In zoos, can only be kept in pairs. The male often carries the young. S America H&B 20cm.

LEMURS, TREE-SHREW, SLOTH

➡ RUFFED LEMUR
Its fur may be a mixture of red, black and white. Makes loud, barking calls when upset. Rare. Madagascar. H&B 60cm.

➡ RING-TAILED LEMUR
May live in big groups. Females are dominant over males. Madagascar. H&B 40cm.

Two claws on front feet

⬅ COMMON TREE-SHREW
Fast mover. Young are left in a nest separate from the mother's. She tends them every few days. S-E Asia. H&B 20cm

⬅ TWO-TOED SLOTH
Sleeps, eats, mates and gives birth upside-down. A slow mover, and very slow on the ground. Eats mainly leaves. S America. H&B 60cm.

GIANT ANTEATER, ELEPHANTS

➡ GIANT ANTEATER
Sleeps for most of the day, its tail curled around it. Has no teeth. Laps up termites with its long, sticky tongue. C & S America. H&B 1m.

⬇ INDIAN ELEPHANT
To keep its skin in good condition, it needs to bathe frequently. All elephants are herbivores. Rare. S-E Asia. SH 3m max.

⬇ AFRICAN ELEPHANT
The largest land animal. Lives in herds with an old female in charge. Adult males live separately. Rare. Africa. SH 4m max.

Small ears and round back

Large ears

DOLPHIN, SEALS

➡ BOTTLE-NOSED DOLPHIN
Like most dolphins, easily bored and may behave unnaturally in zoos as a result. Communicates with whistles and squeaks. Uses echo location to detect distant objects. World-wide. H&B 3.6m max.

Breathes through its blowhole

Ear flaps

Sealions turn their hind limbs forward when walking

⬅ CALIFORNIAN SEALION
Swims by moving its fore-limbs. Its coat appears light fawn when it is dry. The males are called bulls, the females, cows. N Pacific coasts. H&B 2.3m.

Seals' hind limbs are useless on land

➡ GREY SEAL
Seals are not as acrobatic on land as sealions. Try to time how long it stays underwater (up to 15 minutes). Babies have white fur. N Atlantic coasts. H&B 3.1m max.

No ear flaps

ZEBRAS, HORSE, TAPIR

Rump

➡ GRANT'S ZEBRA
Zebras have different rump patterns. **Grevy's Zebras** (rare) bray like donkeys; **Chapman's** and **Grant's** bark; **Mountain zebras** (rare) neigh. **All:** Africa. SH 1.1m.

Mountain zebra

Grevy's zebra

Chapman's zebra

Stiff mane —

⬅ PRZEWALSKI'S HORSE/ TAKH
Pronounced "pshuh-vaal-ski". The only living wild horse, saved from extinction by breeding in zoos. Mongolia. SH 1.1m.

White muzzle

➡ MALAYAN TAPIR
Herbivore. Uses its long lips to pluck food. Feet are specialized for swampy ground and get sore on hard ground. Rare. S-E Asia. SH 1.1m.

RHINOCEROS, HIPPOPOTAMUS

➡ INDIAN RHINOCEROS
Has only one horn. Herbivore browser. Rare. S Asia. SH 2m max.

➡ BLACK RHINOCEROS
Left Hide is dark grey. Rare. Africa. SH 1.7m max.

➡ WHITE RHINOCEROS
Right Hide is slate grey to yellowish brown. Large shoulder hump. Rare. Africa. SH 1.9m max.

Pointed upper lip for browsing

Square upper lip for grazing

⬅ HIPPOPOTAMUS
Spends most of the day in water. Can stay underwater for up to 5 mins. Herbivore. Africa. SH 1.5m.

Large tusks inside mouth

⬅ PYGMY HIPPOPOTAMUS
Its skin secretes an oil that stops it drying out on land. Rare. W Africa. SH 1m.

PECCARY, CAMEL, LLAMA

➡ PECCARY

Not a true pig. If excited, hair over a scent gland near the tail base sticks up and you will smell a musky scent. The young are reddish with a black back-stripe. C & S America. SH 50cm.

Scent gland

⬅ BACTRIAN CAMEL

A two-humped camel from Asia. The **dromedary** from Arabia has one hump. Both are used for riding and carrying loads. Humps store fat, which is used if there is no food. SH 1.8m.

Protective skin on the knees

Very mobile ears for good hearing

➡ LLAMA

Related to camels and, like them, may spit when angry. Its wild ancestor is the **guanaco**, like a slender llama with a red-brown coat. S America. SH 1.2m.

GIRAFFE, OKAPI

Both the male and female have horns, sometimes four or five.

➡ GIRAFFE

The world's tallest animal. Lips and long tongue used to pluck leaves. Gentle, but can give a nasty kick. Mostly silent, but can moo or grunt. Usually sleeps standing up. Africa.
SH 3.1m.
H&B 5m.

The lower jaw moves from side to side when the giraffe eats.

These are some of the other coat patterns you may see.

Due to its long neck, the giraffe must spread its front legs apart to stoop and drink.

♂

⬅ OKAPI

The giraffe's only living relative, discovered in 1901. Its blue-black tongue is long enough to reach its ears. The male has tiny horns covered by skin. Rare. Congo region, Africa. SH 1.6m. H&B 1.9m.

DEER

➡ PÈRE DAVID'S DEER
Extinct in the wild, now
only found in zoos. Has
a dark winter coat and
a light summer coat.
Lives in a large herd led
by a stag. Originally from
China. SH 1.1m.

The skin has
been rubbed off
these antlers.

Summer
coat

♂

Both sexes
have antlers

♂

◀ REINDEER
Like all deer, it sheds
its antlers each year.
New ones are covered
with velvety skin, which is
eventually rubbed off. Eats
lichen. Arctic. SH 1.3m.

Broad hooves
for walking on
snow

Antlers

♂

➡ REEVES' MUNTJAC
Male has small antlers.
Holds its head low when
running. Barks when alarmed.
China. (Escaped animals
wild in S England). SH 50cm.

21

ANTELOPES

➡ COMMON ORYX/ GEMSBOK
Like all antelopes, it never
sheds its horns. Africa.
SH 1.2m.

➡ SCIMITAR-HORNED ORYX
Believed to be extinct
in the wild. Sahara,
N Africa. SH 1m.

Both sexes
have horns

⬅ WHITE-BEARDED
BRINDLED GNU/
BLUE WILDEBEEST
Often live in huge herds
which migrate long
distances to find new
pasture. Active day
and night. Africa.
SH 1.2m.

♀

➡ BLACKBUCK
Each herd has
one male
leader. Females
are nervous and
alert the herd
to danger.
S Asia.
SH 80cm.

♂

ANTELOPES, BISON

➡ BLUE DUIKER
Small, shy antelope. Rubs
glands under its eyes
against objects to mark
out its territory. Africa.
SH 40cm.

Gland

Small hump

⬅ GREATER KUDU
The female is smaller
than the male and has
no horns or fringe on
the throat. Mainly a
browser. Africa.
SH 1.6m max.

♂

Large shoulder
hump

➡ AMERICAN
BISON/ "BUFFALO"
Bellows when angry.
Heavy, but can
move fast. Likes
rolling in mud and
dust. Rare. N America.
SH 2m max.

OX, SAIGA, SHEEP, GOAT

➤ MUSK OX
Under its coarse hair is a fine, woolly undercoat. A herd will stand in a line or circle to face an attacker. Rare. Arctic. SH 1.3m.

Large, wide feet

Summer coat ♂

⬅ SAIGA
The male has horns and an inflatable nose. The winter coat is white and shaggy. S Russia. SH 70cm.

➤ BARBARY SHEEP
The only sheep with a throat-fringe. Both sexes have horns. N Africa. SH 1m.

♂

Fringe

Both sexes have horns

♂

All goats have beards

⬅ MARKHOR
The largest wild goat. Lives in herds usually led by an old female. Rare. Himalayas, Asia. SH 1m.

AUSTRALIAN POUCHED MAMMALS

➡ LONG-NOSED POTOROO
Related to the kangaroo.
Builds nests, carrying nest
material with its tail.
Nocturnal. Australia.
H&B 40cm.

◀ WESTERN GREY KANGAROO
Powerful back legs. Can jump a 2m
fence. Like all Australian pouched
mammals, its young are born tiny and
naked. They climb up to the pouch and
develop inside it. Australia. H&B 1.5m.

⬇ RED KANGAROO
Has white face marks
and a pale tail tip.
Australia. H&B 1.5m.

Female is
usually grey.

When sitting, it uses its tail as a prop.

➡ COMMON WOMBAT
Loves digging. Partly nocturnal,
it spends most of the day in its
burrow. Its pouch opens
backwards to keep out
soil. Australia. H&B 1.2m.

RODENTS

➡ CANADIAN BEAVER
The family lives in a "lodge" built of sticks and mud, with an underwater entrance. The main chamber is above water. N America. H&B 1m.

Slaps the water with its tail as an alarm signal

⬅ MARA
Related to the Guinea Pig. When moving quickly, it may hop like a rabbit. Lives in big groups which dig large burrows. S America. H&B 70cm.

Unlike most rodents, the Mara walks on its toes.

➡ BLACK-TAILED PRAIRIE DOG
Ground-living squirrel. Lives in big groups which dig burrows. A group of burrows is called a "town". N America. H&B 30cm.

Long claws used for digging

⬅ SIBERIAN CHIPMUNK
Ground-living squirrel. Very active. Carries food in its large cheek pouches. N Europe; Asia. H&B 10cm.

WOLF, JACKAL, HUNTING DOG, FOX

➡ **GREY WOLF**
Group howling helps attachments form between all the pack members, and warns other packs of their presence. Europe; N America; Asia. H&B 1.2m max.

⬅ **BLACK-BACKED JACKAL**
Lives in pairs. Nocturnal and shy. S & E Africa. H&B 90cm max.

➡ **AFRICAN HUNTING DOG**
Has a strange, hooting call. Lives in groups with a very strict social order. Africa. H&B 1.1m max.

Very strong jaws

Winter coat

Summer coat

⬅ **ARCTIC FOX**
Its thick white winter coat keeps it warm, and makes it hard to see in the snow. Arctic. H&B 78cm max.

HYENA, COATI, MEERKAT, OTTER

➡ SPOTTED/ LAUGHING HYENA

Lives in groups. A powerful predator and scavenger. It "laughs" at mating time. Africa. H&B 85cm.

Strong jaws used to crunch bone

➡ RING-TAILED COATI

Adult females live in groups. Intelligent and skilful with their claws. C & S America. H&B 65cm max.

Uses its tail to balance when climbing

Always sniffing things with its flexible nose

⬅ MEERKAT/ SURICATE

A type of mongoose. Live in big groups in burrows. "Guards" sit upright to look for danger while the pack is feeding. S Africa. H&B 30cm.

Uses its tail as a rudder when swimming

⬅ CANADIAN OTTER

Partly nocturnal. Loves acrobatics in water, but also spends much time on land. N America. H&B 1m.

BEARS

➡ ASIATIC BLACK BEAR
Dangerous, like all bears, killing with one swipe of its paw. Omnivore. C & E Asia. The **American Black Bear** has no white V on its chest. Omnivore. H&B 1.6m max.

Standing on two legs is a threatening sign

Long claws

⬅ BROWN BEAR
Walks on the soles of its feet, like all bears. Large shoulder hump. The **American Grizzly's** fur is often pale at the tips. Europe, Asia. H&B 3m max.

➡ POLAR BEAR
A powerful hunter in the wild. Thick fur and a fat layer beneath its skin keep it warm enough to swim safely in the freezing waters of the Arctic. Rare. Arctic. H&B 2.5m.

The feet have hairy soles.

BEAR, PANDAS

➡ SUN BEAR

A tropical bear which needs a lot of warmth. Nests in trees. Laps up termites with its long tongue. Especially loves wild honey. Omnivore. S-E Asia. H&B 1.4m max.

U-shaped chest marking

Naked soles

Bamboo

⬅ GIANT PANDA

Once thought the closest relative of the Red Panda, it is now classed as a bear. Tends to live alone. Has special pads on its hands to help it grip bamboo, which is its main diet. Scent-marks its territory by rubbing its bottom on the ground. Rare. China. H&B 1.5m.

➡ RED PANDA

Related to the raccoons. Eats bamboo like the Giant Panda. Rare. Himalayas. H&B 65cm max.

CATS

➡ SERVAL
Runs very quickly over short distances, but climbs little. Has a repetitive, yowling cry. Its hearing is acute. Africa. H&B 95cm.

Very large ears

Short tail

Long legs

⬅ WILD CAT
Looks like a domestic cat, but is larger and stronger. Has a broad head and a bushy tail. Mainly nocturnal. Europe, Africa, W Asia. H&B 60cm.

Bushy tail

➡ OCELOT
Like all cats, it scent-marks its territory with urine. Ocelots are an endangered species due to being hunted for their beautiful fur. Rare. C & S America. H&B 1.3m.

⬅ JUNGLE CAT
Can climb, but spends most of its time on the ground. Like most cats, it can retract its claws. This stops them getting blunt. S Asia. H&B 60cm.

31

CATS

➡ PUMA/ COUGAR/ MOUNTAIN LION
Usually silent, but yowls and screams at mating time. Kittens have spots on their backs and sides. N & S America. H&B 2m max.

Ear tufts

⬅ NORTHERN LYNX
Hisses when angry, and two tufts of fur on its throat stick out. In the wild, it grows a thick winter coat. N America; N Europe; N Asia. H&B 1.3m max.

Winter coat

➡ CARACAL
Live alone. They jump and climb very well. The ear tufts are believed to be used for signalling. Mainly nocturnal. Africa; W Asia. H&B 70cm.

Ear tufts

Short tail

Very long, thick tail

⬅ CLOUDED LEOPARD
An excellent climber, it can hang upside-down from branches by its hind feet. Nocturnal. Rare. S-E Asia. H&B 95cm.

Short legs

Thick winter coat

➡ SNOW LEOPARD
Purrs, but does not roar.
On cold nights, it
wraps its long tail
around its body to
keep its head and
nose warm. Rare.
C Asia. H&B 1m.

Rosette spots

⬅ LEOPARD
Can leap great
distances. Usually
silent, but may make
a coughing noise.
Asia. H&B 1.5m.

⬇ BLACK PANTHER
A dark brown form of
the leopard. Africa;
Asia. H&B 1.5m.

The spots are
still visible

There are black spots
inside the rosettes

➡ JAGUAR
Not a fast runner, but
an excellent swimmer. It
lives near rivers, preying
on animals that come to
drink. There are also
black jaguars. C & S
America. H&B 1.8m.

Short legs

33

CATS

➡ LION
Unlike all other cats,
it lives in big groups,
called "prides".
Most of the time it
rests. The females
do most of the
hunting. Africa;
S-W Asia.
H&B 2.5m max.

Female has
no mane

♂

⬅ TIGER
The largest cat. Lives
alone. Swims very well.
There are several races
(permanent varieties)
varying in colour and
size. The **White Tiger**, for
example has white fur
with stripes. Very rare.
Asia. H&B 3m max.

➡ CHEETAH
The fastest land animal
over short distances. It
can reach speeds of
110 kph. The cubs
have a silver
mane down
their backs.
Rare. Africa.
H&B 2m max.

Can only retract
its claws partially

FLIGHTLESS BIRDS

➡ EMU
Has "hairy" feathers. Like
the Cassowary, the male
Emu keeps the eggs
warm and rears the
young without help
from the female.
Australia.
TL 2m.

Three
toes

♂

♀

Unlike other
birds, it has
only two
toes

⬅ OSTRICH
The largest bird. Runs
very fast on its long,
powerful legs. A male
lives with several
females, which lay
eggs in the same nest.
It is usually the male
that keeps the eggs
warm. Africa. TL 2.4m.

**➡ AUSTRALIAN
CASSOWARY**
One of its three toes has
a long, dagger-like claw,
which it uses for fighting.
It usually lives alone.
Australia. TL 1.5m.

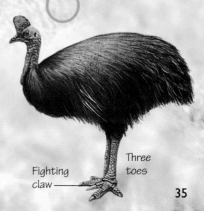

Fighting
claw

Three
toes

35

FLAMINGOS, GOOSE

➡ GREATER FLAMINGO
All flamingos live in large groups. They feed by holding their heads upside-down and sifting water through their bills. Asia; Mediterranean. TL 1.4m.

⬇ LESSER FLAMINGO
The smallest flamingo. Pinker than the Greater Flamingo. E Africa. TL 1m.

Lots of black on bill

➡ CHILEAN FLAMINGO
Left Pale pink. All flamingo chicks are white or grey. S America. TL 1m.

➡ CARIBBEAN/ ROSY FLAMINGO
Right Deep pink or red. Caribbean coasts; Galapagos Islands. TL 1.2m.

⬅ NÉ NÉ/ HAWAIIAN GOOSE
Nearly became extinct, but zoo-bred birds are now being released into the wild. Hawaii. TL 73cm max.

PENGUINS, DUCK, IBIS

➡ KING PENGUIN
Males and females take turns to
incubate eggs. Penguins cannot
fly, but swim superbly.
Antarctic. TL 94cm.

**➡ AFRICAN/
JACKASS PENGUIN**
Makes a braying,
croaking noise. Sub-
Antarctic; S African
coast. TL 72cm.

➡ ROCKHOPPER PENGUIN
As its name implies, it moves
by hopping between rocks.
Antarctic & Sub-Antarctic. TL 56cm.

"Sail" feathers
are lost in
summer

♂

⬅ MANDARIN DUCK
The male uses his bright
colours and "sail" feathers to
court the dull brown female.
They perch and nest in trees.
China. TL 43cm.

➡ SCARLET IBIS
Like many birds, it
often washes bits of
food in its drinking
water before eating.
S America. TL 58cm.

Beak turns
black in the
breeding season

CRANE, STORK, PELICAN

➡ CROWNED CRANE

In spring, watch for their courtship dance. Both sexes flap their wings and leap into the air with loud cries. They may pair for life. They mainly eat small mammals, such as mice. E Africa. TL 1.1m.

◀ MARABOU STORK

One of the largest storks. Usually silent, but like most storks, it rattles its bill loudly when courting. In the wild it eats carrion (dead meat). Africa. TL 1.3m.

Function of the neck pouch is unknown

➡ EUROPEAN WHITE PELICAN

Lives in large groups. Uses its bill and skin pouch as a scoop for catching fish. Waddles on land, but can swim and fly well. E Europe; Asia; S Africa. TL 1.5m.

Skin pouch

Webbed feet. Four forward-facing toes.

PHEASANTS, GUINEAFOWL

➡ INDIAN PEAFOWL
A type of pheasant.
Only the male
(peacock) has long
feathers. He fans them
out and shakes them
when courting the
female (peahen).
India. TL 2m.

**➡ GOLDEN
PHEASANT**
The male displays to
the brown female by
spreading his ruff
feathers and golden
wings. W China.
TL 1m.

*Pheasants lose their
long "covert" feathers
(see below) after the
mating season.*

◀ LADY AMHERST'S PHEASANT
As with all pheasants, what looks
like the tail is really a collection of
long "covert" feathers. The true
tail is hidden beneath them.
China. TL 1.5m.

**➡ HELMETED
GUINEAFOWL**
Listen for its noisy, metallic
cry. Africa. TL 55cm.

39

OWLS, CARACARA

Female is slightly larger than the male

♀

♂

➡ SNOWY OWL
Unlike most owls, it is active during the day. Its white feathers camouflage it against the Arctic snows. Arctic. TL 56cm.

➡ SPECTACLED OWL
Lives near water. The young are white with a black "mask". C & S America. TL 45cm.

Feather-tufts

⬅ EURASIAN EAGLE OWL
A large owl. Its feather-tufts are not ears. They help owls recognize each other. Flies quietly, like all owls. Europe; N Africa; Asia. TL 71cm max.

➡ CARACARA/ CARRION HAWK
Its strong beak and claws are used for tearing dead meat. S America. TL 55cm.

EAGLES

➡ EUROPEAN GOLDEN EAGLE

Like most birds of prey, the female is larger than the male. Mating pairs stay together for life. Prey is caught with powerful claws and carried off for eating. Europe. TL 78cm.

Colour and size vary with habitat and age

Hooked beak

⬅ AFRICAN FISH EAGLE

Dives from treetops to catch fish. Like most birds of prey, it has excellent vision. It throws back its head when making its distinctive, screeching call. Africa. TL 74cm.

Very long, pointed wings

➡ BATELEUR EAGLE

When hunting in the wild, it can glide for hours on its long wings. Has a spectacular courtship display in the air. Africa. TL 64cm.

Short tail

VULTURES, CONDOR

➡ GRIFFON VULTURE

Vultures feed on carrion (dead meat). They have bald heads, as feathers would get matted with blood during feeding. Europe; S-W Asia; S Africa. TL 1.1m max.

Hooked beak used for tearing meat

⬅ KING VULTURE

Like all New World vultures, both sexes circle each other, during courtship, whistling and flapping their wings. Unlike many birds, it is believed to use its sense of smell to find food. C & S America. TL 80cm.

Comb

Wattles

Female has no comb or wattles

➡ ANDEAN CONDOR

Stretches out its wings to warm them in the sun. Wingspan of over 3m. Female has red eyes. S America. TL 1.3m max.

PARROTS

➡ SULPHUR-CRESTED COCKATOO

Screams when excited. May live in large flocks in the wild. Both sexes have crests, and raise them as signals – especially the male at mating time. Australia. TL 50cm.

Crest

⬅ AFRICAN GREY PARROT

Very intelligent. Excels at mimicking voices. Long-lived, like most parrots, often reaching 50 years. Lives in large flocks in the wild. C & W Africa. TL 33cm.

➡ BLUE AND YELLOW MACAW

Left S America. TL 86cm.

➡ SCARLET MACAW

Right C & S America. TL 85cm. All macaws grip hard fruit and nuts with their claws and peel them, or crack them open, with their strong, hooked beaks. They nest in the hollows of trees.

43

PARROTS

➡ YELLOW-BACKED LORY
Like most parrots, it nests in
tree-holes. Lories differ from
Lorikeets in having short tails.
Moluccas, Indonesia.
TL 30cm.

⬅ RAINBOW LORIKEET
Its special tongue helps it to eat
pollen and nectar. It also eats
fruit, leaves, etc. Very noisy.
 Australasia. TL 26cm.

➡ CRIMSON ROSELLA
Eats mainly seeds.
Spends a lot of time
on the ground. S & E
Australia. TL 36cm.

⬅ FISCHER'S LOVEBIRD
Pairs of lovebirds sit closely
together. They groom
each other a lot. In the
wild they live in flocks.
E Africa. TL 15cm.

TOUCANS, TURACO, MINAH, HORNBILL

➡ ARIEL TOUCAN
Orange beak

➡ SULPHUR-BREASTED TOUCAN
Green beak
Large, lightweight beaks help toucans pick fruit off trees. S America. TL 52cm.

Crest——

Red flight feathers

⬅ WHITE-CHEEKED TURACO
Dips as it flies. Has strong feet for jumping and running along branches. W Africa. TL 42cm.

Lightweight beak and horny casque

➡ GREAT INDIAN HORNBILL
At nesting time, the female walls herself into a hole, leaving a slit through which the male feeds her. S-E Asia. TL 1.2m.

⬅ NEPAL HILL MINAH
Can mimic voices well. Becomes aggressive at nesting time. S-E Asia. TL 31cm.

45

ROLLER, PIGEON, MOTMOT, KOOKABURRA

➡ LILAC-BREASTED ROLLER
Named for its rolling, wheeling flight. Mates in the air. Hunts from a perch, taking the food back to the same perch. Africa. TL 36cm.

➡ BLUE-CROWNED PIGEON
Largest pigeon in the world. Feeds on the ground, but flies off if alarmed. New Guinea. TL 68cm.

Saw-edged beak

⬅ BLUE-CROWNED MOTMOT
Sits for long periods on its perch. Central parts of its tail feathers are worn bare from preening and rubbing against objects. C & S America. TL 45cm.

The upper side of the tail is blue

➡ KOOKABURRA/ LAUGHING JACKASS
Cackling call. Kills small prey by banging them against a branch. Australia. TL 46cm.

WHYDAH, STARLING, FINCHES

➤ PARADISE WHYDAH
Lays eggs in the nests of other birds. The male has two long tail feathers in the breeding season. Africa. TL 40cm.

♂ Breeding plumage

➤ PURPLE GLOSSY STARLING
Noisy and aggressive. All starlings are good at mimicking sounds. They sometimes mimic other birds. Africa. TL 22cm.

◄ GOULDIAN FINCH
There are several different colour patterns. Like other grass-finches, both sexes help to keep the eggs warm. Australia. TL 14cm.

♂

➤ BLACK-HEADED WEAVER
Nests in groups, each pair building a nest woven from grass, suspended from a branch. W Africa. TL 15cm.

♂

Entrance

CONSTRICTING SNAKES

→ ANACONDA
Non-poisonous. Spends a lot of time in water. All the snakes on this page are **constrictors** – they suffocate their prey. S America. TL 11.5m max.

Snakes have no outer ear parts

← BOA CONSTRICTOR
Non-poisonous. Can climb. Its tail is slightly prehensile. Mainly nocturnal. C & S America. TL 5.5m max.

All constrictors can open their mouths very wide to swallow large prey

→ INDIAN PYTHON
There are about 20 python species. All non-poisonous. They lay eggs (anacondas and boas bear live young). S-E Asia. TL 7.6m max. **African python**. TL 5.5m max. **Reticulated python**. S-E Asia. TL 10m max. **Royal/Ball python**. Curls into a ball if frightened. W Africa. TL 1.3m max. **Carpet python**. New Guinea; Australia. TL 4.3m max.

African python

Royal python

Reticulated python

Carpet python

POISONOUS SNAKES

➡ GREEN MAMBA
Lives in branches. Moves quickly.
Like all snakes, it swallows its prey
whole. Lays eggs. Africa. TL 2.4m max.

Prehensile tail

Warning
position

Hood

Head without
hood expanded

⬅ INDIAN COBRA
If frightened, its neck
ribs move, expanding
the skin to form a hood.
It may then strike.
S Asia. TL 1.8m max.

➡ PUFF ADDER
A viper. If frightened,
it puffs up to look
threatening. All vipers bear
live young. Africa. TL 90cm.

All vipers
hiss when
frightened

➡ GABOON VIPER
Strikes from a coiled
position. Long front
fangs are folded
back until it actually
strikes. Africa. TL 1.2m.

Rattle

⬅ EASTERN
DIAMONDBACK
RATTLESNAKE
Shakes "rattle" on the
end of its tail to give a
warning. E USA. TL 1.5m.

LIZARDS

➡ COMMON IGUANA
Has sharp claws and climbs well. Will lash out at an enemy with its long, powerful tail. C & S America. TL 1.3m max.

➡ COMMON CHAMELEON
Skin colour changes if it is excited, or if the light or temperature alter. Mediterranean. TL 30cm max.

Prehensile tail

Shoots out a long, sticky tongue to catch insects

◀ STUMPY-TAILED/ SHINGLEBACK SKINK
Slow mover. Lives in the desert. Stores fat in its tail, like many desert reptiles. Australia. TL 45cm max.

➡ LEOPARD GECKO
Fast mover. Climbs well using special gripping pads on its feet. S Asia. TL 30cm max.

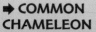

Lashes its tail when angry

◀ NILE MONITOR
Good swimmer. Sharp claws for climbing, digging and defence. Tears its food with sharp teeth. Africa. TL 1.8m.

CROCODILE, ALLIGATOR, TURTLE, TORTOISE

➡ NILE CROCODILE

Keeps very still most of the time, but can move quickly. Can stay underwater for over an hour. Africa. TL 5m max.

Fourth tooth of lower jaw visible when mouth is shut

⬅ AMERICAN ALLIGATOR

Has a broader snout than a crocodile. Eggs laid in large mound-shaped mud nests. The young are black with yellow markings. S-E USA. TL 6m max.

➡ HAWKSBILL TURTLE

Eats sponges. Leaves the ocean to lay eggs. Very rare. Tropical oceans. SL 91cm max.

Beak-like mouth

⬅ GIANT TORTOISE

May live to a great age. Very rare. Galapagos Islands, Pacific Ocean. SL 1.5m max.

NOCTURNAL ANIMALS

➡ SENEGAL BUSHBABY/ GALAGO
Has finger-pads to grip branches.
Strong back legs. Can leap over
2m upwards. Africa. H&B 17cm.

Ears can move
separately or
be folded back

Superb
night vision

⬅ TARSIER
Like an owl, it can hardly
move its huge eyes, but
can turn its head to
look over its shoulder.
S-E Asia. H&B
12.5cm.

➡ COLUGO/ FLYING LEMUR
Not a lemur, but in an order of
its own. It glides between the
rainforest trees on its special
skin-flaps. S-E Asia.
H&B 37.5cm.

Sharp claws help
it to climb

⬇ LARGE FRUIT BAT/
MALAYAN FLYING FOX
Unlike most bats, fruit bats have no echo-
location sense. Has acute hearing and
eyesight, but cannot fly in total darkness.
S-E Asia. H&B 40cm. Wingspan 2m max.

➡ NAKED MOLE RAT
Hardly any hair. Sensitive whiskers on snout. Long front teeth used for tunnelling. Lives in underground colonies with a strict social order. Only one female and 1-3 males are involved in mating. E Africa. H&B 10.4cm.

No ear-flaps

➡ JERBOA
Lives in deserts. Its hind legs are much longer than its front legs. Can cover 3m in one bound. Gets all the water it needs from eating roots and seeds. N Africa; Asia. H&B 15cm max.

Long tail aids balance

⬇ KANGAROO RAT
Like the jerboa, it lives in deserts, moves by hopping, and needs little water. Acute hearing. Camouflaged well in the desert by its sandy coloration. Stores food in cheek pouches. N America. H&B 16cm max.

White stripe on hips

➡ NORTH AMERICAN PORCUPINE
A rodent, like all the animals on page 53. If attacked, it will turn around and thrust the long quills on its back into the predator. Herbivore. H&B 1m max.

NOCTURNAL ANIMALS

➡ FENNEC FOX
Lives in deserts. Its large
ears lose heat to keep it
cool. Acute hearing. Rests
in a burrow during the day.
N Africa; Sinai; Arabia.
H&B 38.5cm.

⬅ DINGO
Believed to descend from dogs
brought to Australia by Aboriginal
settlers. Has short, soft, yellowish to
reddish-brown hair. It yelps and
howls, but does not usually bark.
Australia. H&B 90cm.

➡ NORTH AMERICAN RACCOON
Lives in woods, but will enter towns
to seek food. Likes to wash its
food. Climbs and swims well.
Omnivore. N & C America.
H&B 57.5cm.

Nimble, hand-
like forepaws

Tail raised as
a threat

⬅ STRIPED SKUNK
Raises its tail to warn predators away.
If this fails, it releases a foul smell from
a scent gland under its tail.
N America. H&B 38.5cm.

➡ INDIAN/ GREY MONGOOSE

Brave. Kills and eats cobras. Not immune to their venom, but very agile, and can resist several bites. Asia; Arabia. H&B 30cm.

Thick, protective fur

➡ AARDVARK

No front teeth. Laps up termites with its sticky 40cm tongue. Spends the day in a burrow. Coat varies from sparse and sandy to full, glossy black. C & S Africa. H&B 1.2m max.

Large claws used to break into termite mounds

⬅ PANGOLIN/ SCALY ANTEATER

Greenish scales made of modified hair. Uses claws and tongue, like the aardvark, to hunt termites, but is toothless. Rolls into a ball if threatened. Some pangolin species live in trees. Africa; S-E Asia. H&B 90cm max.

➡ ECHIDNA/ SPINY ANTEATER

Lays an egg, which is kept in a pouch. In danger, it burrows down, leaving only its spikes showing. Australia; New Guinea. H&B 78cm max.

NOCTURNAL ANIMALS

➡ KOALA
It gets all the water it
needs from its sole
diet of eucalyptus
leaves. Carries young
in a pouch. When
older, the young
travel by gripping
their parent's back.
Australia. H&B 78.5cm.

⬅ BOODIE
A type of Rat Kangaroo. Carries
young in a pouch. Eats fruit, bulbs and
seeds. W Australia. Rare. H&B 28cm.

➡ BROWN KIWI
The only bird with nostrils
that open at the tip of its beak.
Used to sniff out worms under the soil.
Its egg is huge in relation to its body.
Flightless. New Zealand. TL 50cm.

Black and white pattern
camouflages it against
the forest canopy.

⬅ SPOTTED LINSANG
Tree-dwelling civet. Like a cat, it
pounces on its prey and can retract
its claws. Feeds on insects, birds and
small mammals. S Asia. H&B 38cm.

VERY RARE ANIMALS

A number of the animals in this book, such as the Tiger, are rare in the wild. Sometimes they are few because of competition with other animals, but more often it is due to hunting by humans, or destruction of their habitat as human industry grows. Many of the animals in this section are so rare you may not see them, even in a zoo.

➡ EASTERN QUOLL
Pouched Australian mammal. Female may have up to 30 young in a litter. Only six usually survive. S-E Australia. H&B 45cm max.

Large ears give acute hearing

⬅ BILBY/ RABBIT-EARED BANDICOOT
Lives in a burrow during the day. Young are carried in a backward-opening pouch. Australia. H&B 55cm max.

➡ GIANT ARMADILLO
Related to anteaters and sloths. Feeds on termites. Its bony plates form a flexible shell. Balances on its hind legs and tail to reach the tops of termite mounds. C & S America. H&B 1m max.

Large claws for burrowing, and breaking into termite mounds

VERY RARE ANIMALS

➡ CARIBBEAN MANATEE
No hind legs. Lives in both fresh and sea water. Active day and night. Herbivore. Coasts of Caribbean, E Mexico & S-E USA. H&B 3.25m.

⬅ GOLDEN LION TAMARIN
Uses its long, clawed fingers to dig insects out of cracks in bark. Lives in family groups. All members help to care for the young. Omnivore. S-E Brazil. H&B 36.6cm max.

➡ HYACINTH MACAW
The largest parrot. Lives in large flocks. Cracks open palm nuts with its powerful beak. The beak is also used to aid climbing. S America. TL 1m.

⬇ KAKAPO
The rarest and heaviest parrot. A nocturnal, flightless, solitary herbivore. To attract mates, males gather in hollows, inflate their chests and boom loudly. New Zealand. TL 60cm max.

WORLD MAP

KEY TO MAP

North America
- USA
- Mexico

South America
- Brazil

Europe
- England
- Russia

Africa
- Ethiopia
- Madagascar

Asia
- China
- Mongolia
- India
- Malaysia
- Indonesia

Australasia
- Australia
- New Zealand

1. Caribbean Sea
2. Mediterranean Sea
3. Sahara Desert
4. Congo Region
5. Sinai
6. Arabia
7. Himalayas

These geographical regions are used in this book:

Sub-Antarctic The area immediately surrounding the Antarctic circle.

Tropical The warm region between the Tropics of Cancer and Capricorn.

Sub-tropical The area immediately surrounding the Tropical region.

WILDLIFE WEß SITES

ANIMALS

African Wildlife Foundation
www.awf.org

Animal Bytes
www.seaworld.org/animal_bytes/
animal_bytes.html

Animal Diversity Web
animaldiversity.ummz.umich.edu

Animal Omnibus
www.birminghamzoo.com/ao

AustralianWildlife.com
www.australianwildlife.com.au

BBC Online Nature
www.bbc.co.uk/nature

Bears.org
www.bears.org

Discovery.com
www.discovery.com

Elephant Information Repository
elephant.elehost.com

NatureExplorer.com
www.natureexplorer.com

Pete & Barb's Penguin Pages
ourworld.compuserve.com/home
pages/peter_and_barbara_barham

The Tiger Information Centre
www.5tigers.org

The Ultimate Ungulate Page
www.ultimateungulate.com

Wolf Country
www.wolfcountry.net

R-Zu-2-U Animal FAQs
www.rzu2u.com/faq.htm

The Bear Den
www.nature-net.com/bears

The Owl Pages
www.owlpages.com

CONSERVATION

Animals of the Rainforest
www.animalsoftherainforest.com

Bagheera's Lair
www.bagheera.com

Bald Eagle Information
www.baldeagleinfo.com

Endangered TV
www.endangeredtv.com

Kakapo Recovery Programme
www.kakaporecovery.org.nz

Monkey World
www.monkeyworld.org

**Royal Society for the
Protection of Birds**
www.rspb.org.uk

Wildlife Conservation Society
www.wcs.org

World Wide Fund for Nature
www.panda.org

WILDLIFE PARKS & ZOOS

The Good Zoo Guide Online
www.goodzoos.com

Zoo Net
www.zoonet.org

Auckland Zoo (NZ)
www.aucklandzoo.co.nz/index.php

Barcelona Zoo (Spain)
www.zoobarcelona.com/zoo_ingles/
presentacio.htm

Belfast Zoo (N Ireland)
www.belfastzoo.co.uk

Bronx Zoo (USA)
www.bronxzoo.com

Brookfield Zoo (USA)
www.brookfieldzoo.org

Busch Gardens Zoo (USA)
www.buschgardens.org

Chester Zoo (UK)
www.demon.co.uk/chesterzoo

Dublin Zoo (IRE)
www.dublinzoo.ie

Edinburgh Zoo (UK)
www.edinburghzoo.org.uk

Hannover Zoo (GER)
www.zoo-hannover.de/home_e.html

Minnesota Zoo (USA)
www.mnzoo.org

Montréal Biodôme (CAN)
www.ville.montreal.qc.ca/biodome/
ebdm.htm

Paignton Zoo (UK)
www.paigntonzoo.org.uk

Philadelphia Zoo (USA)
www.phillyzoo.org

Phoenix Zoo (USA)
www.phoenixzoo.org/zoo

**San Diego Zoo & San Diego
Wild Animal Park** (USA)
www.sandiegozoo.org

St Louis Zoo (USA)
www.stlzoo.org

Taronga Zoo Sydney (AUS)
www.zoo.nsw.gov.au

Victoria's Three Zoos (AUS)
www.zoo.org.au

Woodland Park Zoo (USA)
www.zoo.org/index2.html

Zoo Atlanta (USA)
www.zooatlanta.org

MAPS

National Geographic Maps
www.nationalgeographic.com/maps/

WorldAtlas.com
www.worldatlas.com/aatlas/
world.htm

USEFUL WORDS

browser - an animal that eats mainly the leaves of trees and bushes.

canine teeth - long, sharp teeth at each side of the jaws, used to seize prey.

carnivores - meat eaters. *Carnivora* - an order of mammals with teeth specialized for eating flesh, for example, lions.

class - an animal group within a phylum, for example, the mammals.

conservation - the efforts made to protect nature in order to safeguard the future of all living things.

echo location - the ability of animals such as bats to locate objects by detecting echoes bouncing off them.

family - an animal group within an order, such as the *Felidae* (Cats).

genus - an animal group within a family, such as *Panthera* (Big Cats).

grazer - an animal that eats mainly grasses.

grooming - animals keeping themselves, or each other, clean by licking, or picking off insects.

habitat - the area in which an animal naturally lives.

herbivores - plant eaters.

mammals - a class of hairy, warm-blooded animals that suckle their young with milk.

marsupials - a group of mammals that suckle their young in a pouch.

omnivores - animals that eat both plants and meat.

order - an animal group within a class, for example, the *Carnivora*.

phylum - any of the largest divisions of the Animal Kingdom.

prehensile - a term that describes a body part specialized for grasping, such as an elephant's trunk.

rodents (*Rodentia*) - an order of mammals with chisel-shaped front teeth specialized for gnawing, for example, mice.

scent gland - an organ that releases scent, often as a signal to other animals.

species - a specific type of animal within a genus, such as the tiger.

territory - the part of an animal's habitat that it defends as its own.

INDEX